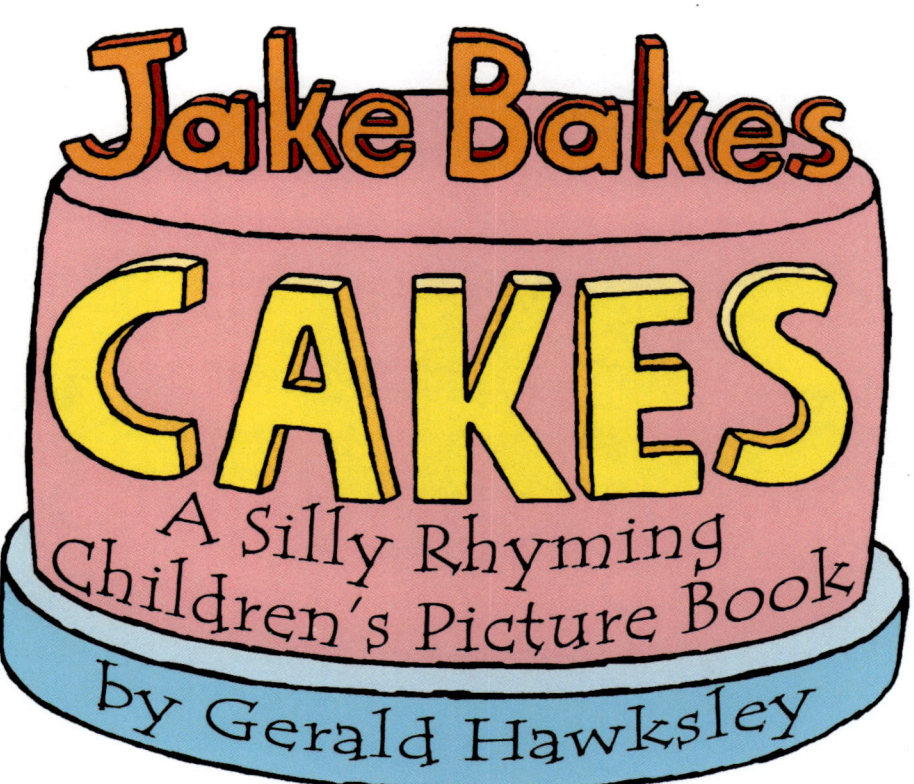

© 2012 Gerald Hawksley
All Rights Reserved.

This is Jake.
Jake bakes cakes!

What kind of cakes does Jake bake?

He bakes upside down cakes for acrobats.

And pumpkin cakes for witches and their cats.

He bakes banana cakes for monkey in the tree.

And fish cakes
for fishes in the sea.

He bakes fairy cakes for pixies in the park.

And scary cakes
for ghosties in the dark.

He bakes birthday cakes
for birthday surprises.

And invisible cakes
for spies in disguises.

He bakes cheese cakes
for mice, of course.

And oat cakes for horse.

He bakes honey cakes
for bears to eat with their paws.

And Christmas cakes for Santa Claus.

He bakes iced cakes
for penguins in the snow.

And squishy cream cakes for clowns to throw.

He bakes carrot cakes for rabbits to munch.

And fruit cakes
for Professor Plum's lunch.

He bakes angel cakes
for balloonists in the sky.

And pink cakes
for pink pig in his sty.

He bakes coffee cakes
to wake up sleepy heads.

And mouldy cakes
for monsters under beds.

He bakes the cup cake
for the winner of the race.

And moon cakes
for astronauts in space.

He bakes wedding cakes as tall as can be.

And short cakes for Tom Thumb
to have with his tea.

He bakes chocolate cakes
for chocolate fans.

And robot's cakes he makes from old cake tins and tin cans.

Those are the kind of cakes that Jake bakes.

And what does Jake do when his baking day is done?

Why, he throws off his hat,
and puts up his feet -

And has a lovely slice of cake to eat!

More silly rhyming picture books
by Gerald Hawksley:

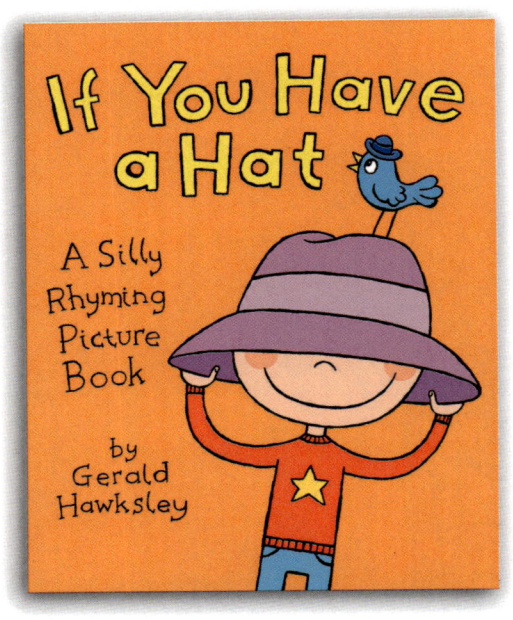
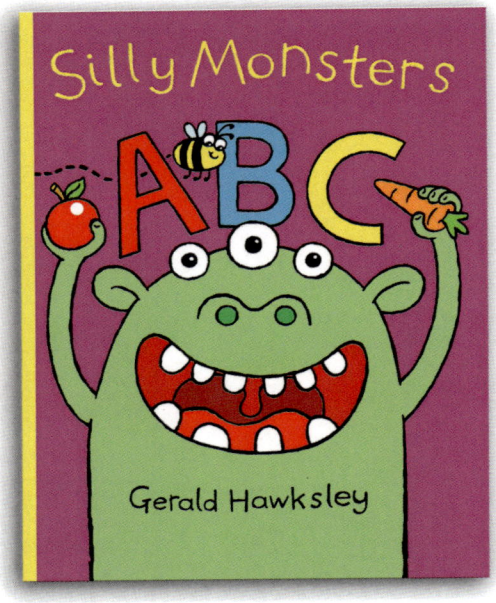

geraldhawksley.com